YOU

Can't Give Up!

Authored

by

Abram Jones

Copyright © 2018 by Abram Jones

ISBN: 9780-578-42538-2

This title is available as an e-book. It is also available via online retailers.

All rights reserved. No part of this publication may be reproduced, stored in a retrieval system or transmitted in any form or by any means-electronic, mechanical, photocopy, record or any other except for brief quotations in printed reviews, without permission from the author/publisher.

Printed in the United States of America.

Scriptural references were taken from various versions of the holy Bible King James Version, New King James Version, New International Version, Message Bible Version, and the Amplified Bible.

Dedication

I dedicate this motivational text to God *first*, and to every person that has considered fainting! Don't you dare give up! God's plan for your life requires some uneasiness - it is preparation for what lies ahead! So, in the moments when defeat rears its ugly head, you can boldly declare, "I recognize you, and with God I was victorious *before* and I know I will be victorious *again,* I refuse to give up now!"

Table of Contents

Introduction iv

Chapters

1   Put in the Work 1

2   You'll Need That Towel 14

3   Man in the Mirror 27

4   Fit Not to Quit 38

5   Better Days Ahead 48

6   Keep Pressing 55

7   Faith Always Wins 61

About the Author 70

Introduction

People decide to give up every day… this means they also decided to start a goal, a project, and eventually, they planned to complete *it*. Oh, how easy it is to simply start something… however, the Glory dwells in the completion of that thing. This literary work is designed to compel, propel, and ultimately tell the readers what is necessary to be an overcomer and not be overcome by the unavoidable trials of life!

No one is exempt from experiencing adversity! However, we are ALL equipped with the required due diligence to overcome hardships, *if* we maintain our faith in God. Fortunately, God sends His messenger(s) to instruct, guide, encourage, and lead His people to their God-ordained purpose!

This literary directive is a message [Don't shoot the messenger]; it will help and motivate anyone who *has* thought about giving-up, *currently contemplating* giving-up, or simply *in need of a little inspiration*. Remember, Goliath saw David in the physical, he couldn't see the spiritual victory that was already manifested! God's got you, that towel in your hand is *your* victory flag… YOU can't give up, not now, not EVER!

Chapter 1
Put in the Work

Over the years, I've encountered numerous people who've contemplated giving up. Their mentalities of defeat were caused by a variety of stressors: their jobs, financial dilemmas, loss of a loved-one, or not achieving a goal at the *mandated* time. Their perspective made their circumstances *seem* insurmountable… truth is we've ALL been there.

Consequently, I understand that *sometimes* the pressures of life produce emotional defeat, which inevitably lead to a domino-effect of unbeneficial reactions instead of provoked and progressive actions.

As a child, I struggled with reading comprehension. Several of my friends *appeared* to be more intelligent than me. In high school, they exceled in Honors and AP courses due to their intellectual aptitude. Therefore, I never told them about my reading difficulties. They were unaware that I simultaneously took remedial *and* honors courses. My honors courses were much more intense compared to what I'd been exposed to. Intellectually, it developed areas of my mind that were not utilized. Although, my coursework *seemed* too difficult, I didn't become discouraged. Obstinately, I KEPT PRESSING!

As fate would have it, when I received my test results for the Florida Comprehensive Assessment Test (FCAT) during my sophomore year of high school, I discovered that I had failed. I became despondent and fearful. Fearful that I may not matriculate to the college of my dreams. Fearful of what my family and friends would say or think of me.

Fearful of receiving a certificate of completion instead of my high school diploma, and an overwhelming fear of being a 'certified' failure.

However, as time passed, I escaped *that* valley of fear. During my junior year of high school, I committed extra time after school with my intensive reading teacher, Ms. Winters. She tutored and helped sharpened areas in my mind that were dull. We studied for countless days.

As a result, after I retook the FCAT, my score exceeded the requirement of passing. How did it happen? I PUT IN THE WORK. I prioritized my time and focused. I understood that proper planning ensured lucrative preparation. Yes, it is true that what we put in is what we'll get out. Nevertheless, our time should be utilized wisely and effectively. Focus on the most important things *first* and favorable result are foreseeable.

> # F.E.A.R. IS FALSE EVIDENCE APPEARING REAL

The biggest fear for most people is failing. Fear is nothing but False Evidence Appearing Real. Thus, we *will* potentially operate from a paralyzed perspective.

The influence of fear, aborts our dreams and leads us to a valley of futility. Fear changes "I can" into "I can't."

Have you ever been in a place where you were faced with a challenge? Consequently, fear caused you to *feel* hopeless? For instance, you've done extremely well on assignments in school, but when an exam was placed in front of you… fear gripped your memory and your ability to perform *well*. What about the times you were selected to speak to a crowd, and you spent countless hours preparing your rhetoric, then when the opportunity presented itself for you to speak, you became nauseated. This is because of fear. The following list details some of the common in life:

1.   **Failure**

We are too timid to try new things because we think we lack the confidence to succeed. When our plans don't materialize as we expected, disappointment settles within and we refuse to try *again*. Don't ever give up because if success doesn't happen initially, keep trying. The fear of failing, transforms into an excuse for unproductiveness. One of my favorite authors, John Maxwell, the internationally renowned leadership expert said it best, "Sometimes We WIN —

Sometimes We ~~Lose~~ Learn!" which simply means learning from our failures makes us winners.

2. **Being Alone**

Loneliness is an emotional state in which a person experiences a powerful feeling of emptiness and isolation. The fear of being alone lulls many people into depression, anxiety, and insecurity.

I often wonder what stimulates individuals to jump from one relationship to another or remain in toxic relationships. I've concluded it is the fear of being alone. Truth is, we must learn how to be happy and discover ways to be genuinely content with ourselves'. Take time to get a better understanding of *your* interests, passions, emotions, dreams, and desires.

3. **Change**

America's meteorological seasons are recognized as spring, summer, fall, and winter. Being a Floridian, there are times we go through all four seasons in one day. As I reminisce a few years ago, in the month of November, I traveled to Madisonville, Tennessee to pick up my godson for the Thanksgiving break. When I left my residence, I wore a pair of khaki shorts, a white V-neck shirt, and flip flops. Once I arrived in the State of Tennessee, I stopped at a gas station. As I unbuckled my seatbelt, I opened the door and the wind closed it. It was bone-chilling cold, *brrrrrrrrrrr*!!!

I needed proper attire. There had been a significant change in temperatures. Although, I was comfortable in my apparel and did not want to change… I realized that in order to stay warm I needed to change.

Many are timid when it comes to change. Consequently, they become complacent, rather than growing and progressing. We live in a rapidly-changing world where many people fear. The trepidation of change can cause an individual to become stationary, unfruitful, and unproductive. Tackle *this* fear by realizing that all change isn't bad!

Genesis 12:1-3:

The Lord had said to Abram, "Go from your country, your people and your father's household to the land I will show you.

² "I will make you into a great nation,
and I will bless you;
I will make your name great,
and you will be a blessing.
³ I will bless those who bless you,
and whoever curses you I will curse;

> *and all peoples on earth*
> *will be blessed through you."*

In order for Abram's promised to be fulfilled, there had to be a change of trajectory and purposeful movement *by* faith. If Abram had not stepped out on faith and moved, he would have compromised his blessings from God. Inherently, we can be very stubborn when it comes to change because we don't like to be uncomfortable.

4. People

The fear of people can cause stagnation. Never allow the negative opinions of others to validate you and keep you boxed into their menial expectations of *you*. David would have never defeated Goliath if he had listened to his brothers discouraging claims. Nehemiah would have never rebuilt the walls of Jerusalem if he had listened to Sanballat. Be keenly perceptive of the people you encounter.

> ## Your Destiny is Calling You

They will either help or hinder you. Don't allow anyone to hinder, intimidate, or manipulate you from stepping into your purpose. You have work to do and your destiny is calling you.

"Care about what other people think and you will always be their prisoner."
-Lao Tzu

The biological term "homeostasis" means having the tendency to go back to a state when destabilized. For our purpose it refers to falling back in the same groove. It's the enemy's job to keep us bound by fear. He knows the minute we step out, he's in trouble.

When overcoming fear, we must be strong and courageous.

According to 2 Timothy 1:7:

For God has not given us a spirit of fear, but of power and of love and of a sound mind.

David once said in Psalm 56:3 *that when I am afraid, I put my trust in God.* You don't have to live in fear, just put in the work and keep working.

2 Corinthians 5:7 declares, *For we walk by faith, not by sight.*

I'm reminded of when God spoke to Joshua after the death of Moses and said:

This is my command—be strong and courageous! Do not be afraid or discouraged. For the Lord your God is with you wherever you go.
-Joshua 1:9 NLT

Joshua would have never succeeded if he remained fearful. He was courageous enough to put in the work and transition from fear to faith. The success we achieve in life is proportional to the quality and the quantity of the effort that we put in. Often times, we know exactly what we need to do, however, we lack the courage and motivation to do it. To be goal achievers, we must figure out how to put in more effort.

Do you have enough courage to tell fear that your trajectory has changed because of your faith? **F.A.I.T.H.** meaning *Fear Ain't In* <u>**This**</u> *House!*

Faith is simply believing that as we navigate through life's journey, we trust God to be our GPS (Global Positioning System). God decreed:

I know what I'm doing, I have it all planned out—plans to take care of you,

not abandon you, plans to give you the future you hope for.

-Jeremiah 29:11 (MSG)

Are you struggling trying to figure out what God has in store for you? Try **following** His plan.

- ✓ Submit to the Lord
- ✓ Stepping out of FEAR and step into FAITH
- ✓ Sanctify your hearts and bodies

If you follow these three steps of faith, you'll discover the Master's plan for your life!

Chapter 2
You'll Need That Towel

  Millions of tourists from around the world visit the beautiful metropolis of Orlando, Florida. They explore, shop, dine, and create everlasting memories. Most of them discover infamous entertainment venues like: B.B. Kings, Universal Studios, City Walk, SeaWorld, and the World's Largest Theme Park, Disney World.

  As a child, I was overly excited when my family vacationed in Orlando and explored Disney's Theme Parks. The parades were amazing. The food was delectable. The electrifying rides such as the Rockin' Roller Coaster, Tower of Terror, and Space Mountain are my all-time favorites.

  Walt Disney had to be a phenomenal visionary to construct such extravagant attractions for families and friends to unite and enjoy each other. I know his vision didn't happen for Walt Disney overnight, he started from somewhere. Walt Disney filed for bankruptcy several times to make his dream a reality. I'm sure there were days and nights where he contemplated on throwing in the towel. Fortunately, he didn't. He believed he could do it and as a result, he achieved it. His setbacks prepared him for tremendous triumphs.

    Setbacks are sudden pauses of forward motion or progress that impose limits or restraints that *can* lead to defeat or reversal of advancement. Expectantly, no one is exempt from experiencing setbacks and no one is usually prepared for the detriment they bring.

For instance, after being on a financially-lucrative job for nearly 15 years, most people don't imagine being terminated, but it happens. Questions like, how will the bills get paid and how will their families be sustained consume their minds.

Perhaps being married to the love of your life for a few years and both of you attained wonderful occupations with great benefits. In addition, you have intelligent beautiful children who are engaged in recreational activities. Everything seems to be going well until one day you discover your loved one's health is declining.

Life blindsides us and sometimes it simultaneously knocks us down; and giving up seems logical. A woman who has discovered her husband's extramarital affair *could* cause her to give up. The teenagers who engaged in consensual sex and as a result the teenage girl became pregnant… she wants to give up! At times, those who work diligently in ministry consider giving up because they feel unappreciated and empty.

According to Genesis 37, Joseph - the eleventh born son of Jacob never anticipated the assault and abandonment from his own brothers coming. Being a dreamer and his father's favorite meant his brothers would be supportive, *right?* No, they hated him because of their father's affection towards him and they did not speak peaceably to him. They planned and plotted to kill him.

Instead, they stripped Joseph of his identity and clothing and cast him into a pit. His situation didn't get any better it got worse. Joseph was falsely accused in the world's first sexual harassment case by Potiphar's wife. My grandmother often said, "If it's not one thing, it's another."

In the midst of being abandoned, sold into slavery, and finally put into prison, Joseph never threw in the towel because God was with him.

When you pass through the waters, I will be with you;
And through the rivers, they shall not overflow you.
When you walk through the fire, you shall not be burned,
Nor shall the flame scorch you.

-Isaiah 43:2

In all that Joseph experienced, God had a higher purpose for his life. He held on to what God had showed him and it came to pass. No good thing will God withhold from the upright. Like Joseph, there are things that appear in our life unexpectedly that cause us to question God's sovereignty. We ask, "God why me?" Life has taught to avoid questioning why, but instead seek the purpose of my trials.

And we know that all things work together for good to them that love God, to those

who are the called according to His purpose.

Romans 8:28

I started a church at the age of 22, The Word Christian Center. We didn't have our own building so we utilized The Women's Coterie Club of Hastings. We loaded and unloaded our equipment on a consistent basis for quite some time. It was toilsome; however, we did it without murmuring or complaining. We knew God had a better plan.

After searching for a location to have our services, we found the *perfect* church, it seated up to 200 people. We believed the church belonged to us. After negotiating with the owner, we discovered that much work needed to be done and that the overall cost would be more than what was listed.

Subsequently I prayed and fasted, the Lord stationed me at The Lord's Temple City of Refuge in Hastings, the church where I grew up singing and dancing until the age of 7. This was a major transition as two churches became one. Bishop, a very humble and generous man brought me in as a pastor and his successor. What a burden release it was especially for Aaron and Quintin who faithfully hauled the sound equipment every week.

The sanctuary was beautiful and over 10,000 square feet, more importantly it was paid for! However, I didn't foresee the challenges ahead. The Bishop and I had disagreements due to indifferences. I didn't understand why he did things a certain way and vice versa. Nevertheless, I remained humble, respectful, and focused. I even asked, "God, what are you doing?" "Why did you put me with this 67-year-old guy?" Doubtfully, more people preyed/prayed against the merge than they prayed for it. Nevertheless, God was for us.

If God is for us, who can be against us?
Romans 8:31b

Even in my misunderstandings about the merge, my confidence was in God. I refused to throw in the towel because I knew I would need it for someone else. The towel that you are carrying isn't really for you, it's for someone else. Someone is facing what you were up against today and you have it in you to share your story.

Their ears need to hear how *you* overcame being molested at a young age. They are waiting to hear *your* story of escaping an abusive relationship and finding love after you thought it *couldn't* happen. They're anticipating *your* success story of after graduating from college you couldn't find a job, but you didn't throw in the towel. You searched and applied and eventually God blessed you!

All things include: the good, bad, and ugly. For things to work out for your good, you must meet the criteria and that is you must:

1. Love God
2. Be called according to His purpose

David had a pretty rough life even though he was man after God's own heart. Although he was king; he committed murder and adultery. 2 Samuel 2:13 states: Then David said to Nathan, "I have sinned against the Lord." Nathan replied, "The Lord has taken away your sin. You are not going to die." David acknowledges that he had sinned and in Psalm 51, David's prayer of repentance to God he asked God to have mercy on him and to purify him from sin. In all that David encountered, the good, the bad, and the ugly, he knew how to go to God because he loved Him.

The number one commandment is that *you should love the Lord your God will all your heart and with all your soul and will all your mind and with all of your strength* (Mark 12:30). Loving God is simply surrendering totally to Him and submitting to His will. 1 John 2:15 teaches us that it's impossible to love God and the world at the same time. When we love God, we obey what He commands and become willing vessels who seeks to please Him. Once we have tasted and have experienced that the Lord is good, we desire more and more of Him.

You intended to harm me, but God intended it all for good. He brought me to

this position so I could save the lives of many people.

-Genesis 50:20

Joseph went through every setback you could ever imagine: family rejection, ostracism, and incarceration. In the midst of the tragedies he faced, he flourished in the end.

Job was one who was perfect and upright experienced evil. He lost everything that God had given to him. He had lost his sheep, his oxen, his camels, his servants, and all of his sons and daughters. His faithless wife tried to tell him to curse God and die. He was tried, tempted, and tested yet, he experienced the good (God) in the end.

According to Job 42:10, God had given him twice as much as he had before.

Nehemiah the prophet had distractions, yet he remained focused and rebuilt the walls of Jerusalem.

Jesus Christ, the Son of the Living God endured such excruciating pain. He was severely beaten and tormented by the Roman soldiers. He was beaten so badly he became unrecognizable. The Prophet Isaiah prophesied this:

But he *was* wounded for our transgressions, *he was* bruised for our iniquities: the chastisement of our peace *was* upon him; and with his stripes we are healed.

-Isaiah 53:5

Jesus Christ was bruised and beaten so we would not have to throw in the towel. Christ paid for our redemption and He died for our deliverance. And on third day, He rose with all power in His hands. Being that He got up, we can get up too. GET UP! You are going to need that towel.

After pastoring for a total of five years in the familiar area I grew up in, God begin to speak to me that it's time to change the course. I'd gotten comfortable and became complacent. After much prayer, I resigned from the pastorate. It was rumored that I had thrown in the towel on my pastoral call. I responded, "No, I'm simply folding the towel." Folding the towel implies that I'm resting in God, waiting on the next assignment. *There will be times where you may have to fold your towel, just don't throw it away.*

Chapter 3
Man in the Mirror

The first thing I do when I wake up in the morning, is look in the mirror just to see how ugly I look after a good night's rest. I'm pretty sure you do the exact same thing, right? RIGHT! If you are woman or anything like my mother, you'll spend hours in the mirror putting on make-up, eye-lashes, fixing your hair, etc.

As a young man, the longest I stand in the mirror is when I'm shaving my head. I examine myself for two reasons. One is so that I don't cut myself and the other is that I don't miss a spot. Sometimes, I still miss leaving a few patches in my head. When we look in a mirror it reflects back a true image of what and who we are. Each morning as we prepare for work or whatever we are to do that day, we generally don't leave without looking in the mirror. The mirror enables us to see if there is anything out of place and gives us a chance to correct the problem.

Michael Jackson, better known as the "King of Pop", was an American singer, dancer, songwriter, and one of the most popular entertainers in the world. He wrote the musical hit "Man in the Mirror" in 1987. Those lyrics directed an electrifying message that in order to make a difference in society, we must do some self-reflection and change inwardly.

According to Psalm 51, David, a man after God's own heart, constantly reflected on his wretchedness. He knew he had problems, he needed to be delivered (daily), and only God could make the necessary changes that needed to occur in his life. He acknowledged his transgressions and asked God to make him better.

Create in me a clean heart, O God; and renew a right spirit within me.

Psalm 51:10

The only way we become better is through confession. Confession leads to transformation. Identity crises do not have age restrictions. However, teenagers experience this type of confusion and frustration quite frequently. Webster defines an identity crisis as a feeling of unhappiness and misunderstanding caused by not being sure about what type of person one really is or the true purpose of one's life.

The teenage years are riddled with significant and puzzling changes of self-discovery. At times, some get lost in the "need" of wanting acceptance.

Typically, they make immature and foolish decisions that they later regret. It is during the adolescent identity crisis that this profound affect *can* linger into adulthood. Thus, some get lost in the discovery process and pretend to be something that they're not.

Are you an individual pretending to be something you're not? Have you suffering from self-deception? Do you know who you *really* are? Who is the man *or* woman in the mirror? If you don't know who you are or *whose* you are, walking in your God-given uniqueness will be difficult! Get to know the "real" you! Look in the mirror [examine yourself] and find *your* true identity.

Holidays usually unite families and friends. During these times that we eat, laugh, and enjoy each other's company. On November 27, 2014, Thanksgiving Day, I chose to stay home alone. It was the first time

I did not surround myself around family and friends during such a *special* time. I was burdened, depressed, and I didn't want to be around anyone.

As I sat in my recliner, suicidal thoughts bombarded my mind. Yes, I had a relationship with God, but I'd felt like giving up. I was overwhelmed with life and felt dissatisfied. My confidence and self-esteem were at an all-time low. Many knew and saw me as the preacher, but no one knew what I was facing inwardly.

Spiritual leaders are often perceived as superhumans! Our humanness is dismissed, and our call is overly glorified and misconstrued as "perfection." We are fallible; we bleed, we hurt, and we cry.

I walked into my grandparent's room and located my grandfather's pistol underneath the bed in a safe. I loaded the gun and cleared the safety. I proceeded back to the living room and sat down in the recliner with the gun. As I attempted to pull the, my phone rang. On the other end was one of my best friends. Deep down, he knew something wasn't right and his response was simply whatever you're thinking of doing, don't do it. He then prayed for me and he made it his business to visit me. God knows what we need it! After crying a bucket of tears, I went to the restroom, looked at myself in the mirror, and I spoke the word of God over my life.

When a person commits suicide, their love ones are taken by surprise. It leaves them with several haunting unanswered questions. Unfortunately, people commit suicide for various reasons and those questions may loom eternally.

However, the most common correlation is linked to depression. Severe depression is always accompanied by a pervasive sense of suffering as well as the belief that escapes from it is hopeless. The state of depression causes warped thinking, and irrational thoughts like: "everyone will be better off without me" to make sense.

Suicidal attempts are a cry for help and the verbal articulation of the individual's pain is overwhelming. Usually they do not want to die, but they want to alert those around them that something is seriously wrong. The ideal example of this is a young teenage girl or boy suffering genuine anxiety because of a relationship, either with a friend, or parent. Practically stated, they need help without criticism or judgment.

Wallowing in mistakes *can* lead to suicidal thoughts. I've made some dreadful mistakes. However, instead of submerging myself in self-pity, I moved forward and learned valuable lessons. My past is behind me and *it* remains there! Today's generation suffers terribly from relieving their mistakes. They tend to discount the needs for life lessons. There is a sense of entitlement and misinformation. Too many of our youth believe that their "struggles" equate to defeat; they don't realize they are still STANDING in the midst of the struggle.

We live in a society with a quick-fix mentality with people that don't want to take no for an answer (especially youth). Rather than trusting in God, we take matters in our own hands because we feel as if God is tardy. Then we become frustrated and have "tantrums" when God's sovereignty overrules our plans.

Having a self-centered mentality or believing the world revolves around you is unhealthy. Here are a few scenarios:

- Rachel wants to hang out with her friends for the weekend. She asks her father for money. He responds that he's unable to do it this weekend due to bills. Rachel now has an insolent demeanor and doesn't speak or acknowledge her father for the entire week.

- Porsha and Ayanna are best friends. One-day Ayanna called Porsha and she didn't answer. Ayanna then deleted Porsha off all her social media sites and blocked her number because Porsha couldn't respond swiftly.

- Juan is a sophomore in college and has taken chemistry twice. If he doesn't pass this time, his tuition will increase to the out-of-state rate. Instead of studying for his final exam, he decided to party with his friends. He became intoxicated and passed out. He was scheduled to take his exam the next day. When the test was placed in front of him, he was unable to function because he was nauseated.

Within a few hours he discovered that he failed again. Sadly, he blamed everyone else except himself.

All of these scenarios highlight a sense of entitlement. Understand *you* may be suffering from self-entitlement if:

- You feel sorry for yourself if things don't work in *your favor*.
- You feel as though everyone is competing *against* you.
- You expect your friends to contribute while *you never invest*.
- You've become egotistical and feel as if the *spotlight should remain on you*.
- You despise when someone disagree with you. Therefore, you try to turn others against that individual with backlashing and gossiping.

- You *impose demands* on everyone you encounter.

The Man in the Mirror starts with you. You must relinquish the entitlement mentality. Everyone must grow up and realize no one is required *to give you* what you want or need. You must be a go getter and get it yourself. Stop looking for and expecting handouts. Work hard and pray harder! Furthermore, stop complaining. Be grateful. Ungratefulness stagnates your growth. Finally, don't depend on others to bail you out. You've been dependent long enough, allow God to teach you how to be independent.

Chapter 4
Fit Not to Quit

Therefore we also, since we are surrounded by so great a cloud of witnesses, let us lay aside every weight, and the sin which so easily ensnares us, and let us run with endurance the race that is set before us, ² looking unto Jesus, the author and finisher of our faith, who for the joy that was set before Him endured the cross, despising the shame, and has sat down at the right hand of the throne of God. - **Hebrews 12:1-2**

The thought of becoming fit requires training. If you're thinking about becoming a boxer or a wrestler, you must be trained. Never underestimate your opponent and you must be prepared for the fight. Training and preparation are vital components of success!

Most people assume that thin individuals with high metabolism can eat anything without gaining weight. I *thought* it was true as well. I love food and I love sweets.

However, I had to ask myself, "Is my diet healthy?" At 23, I begin to challenge myself by eating better and exercising. I set a goal to gain twenty pounds of muscle mass. I realized I needed to put some meat on my bones.

I've had gym memberships with LA Fitness and Planet Fitness. I always *started* well, I was excited and consistent for about 2-3 weeks with my diet and exercise regimen, then I'd just stop!

The proof of my inconsistency was on my bank statement, I wasted money due to my lack of commitment. I hated knowing that $20-$25 was deducted from my account every month and I had nothing to show for it. Yes, it is true; we can become easily sidetracked in trying to obtain a goal. I did not know how to manage everything that I was doing, so I procrastinated and became lackadaisical.

"Don't have too many irons in the fire."- Persian Proverb

Years passed, and I decided to tackle fitness goals *again* and I joined Bailey's Fitness. I'd learned how to better prioritize my daily agenda. I followed Jim Stoppani's Shortcut to Size Plan. I set my schedule and my exercise routine and I committed to it!

- ✓ Day 1- Chest, Triceps, and Calves
- ✓ Day 2- Back, Biceps, and Abs
- ✓ Day 3- Active Rest
- ✓ Day 4- Shoulders, Traps, and Calves
- ✓ Day 5- Legs and Abs
- ✓ Day 6- Active Rest
- ✓ Day 7- Active Rest

Dear friend, I know that you are spiritually well. I pray that you're doing well in every other way and that you're healthy. – 3 John 2:2

Due to my consistency, I've made progress because I was determined to finish what I have started. I realized the importance of being fit physically. My uncle Abe once told me that it's good to have plan on what you will work on at the gym, but eating right plays a major factor. I did just that, I limited the intake of sweets and unhealthy foods and I saw the benefit of my efforts.

We are all guilty of procrastinating at some point or other. The worst thing about procrastinating is that it highlights stagnation and complacency. It causes us to miss out on opportunities that could have been life changing. In a world that is constantly evolving, sometimes we want to change, but we don't know how to take a step forward. Obviously, something is in the way and we must uncover the root of our procrastination.

A friend of mine struggled deeply with low self-esteem. I found out that procrastination doesn't emphasize this, it actually worsens it. He constantly beat himself up about everything and asked, "Why can't I do this?" You can never become fit to not quit if you succumb to the lies of a poor self-image and low self-esteem. It limits you and makes you feel unreasonably inferior. He had great ideas, but nothing flourished. Procrastination slowly ate away his confidence. Fortunately, he decided to focus on building his self-esteem and thus he started to *grow again*. Procrastination cannot we remain in a place of forward movement! My friend is thriving and now understands *who* he is and *whose* he is.

> **"Procrastination is opportunity's assassin."- Victor Kiam**

Your mentality must shift in order to become fit. You must change the way you think. Your mind is the place of your intellect, reasoning, and intentions. Everything starts in the mind. It's the adversary's objective to muddle with your thinking. If he or anyone else can infiltrate your intellect with pessimistic thoughts, then it *will* be impossible for you to become fit mentally.

- **Watch who you *ALLOW* in your ear.**
- **Watch who you *CONFIDE* in.**
- **Watch who you give *PROXIMITY* to.**

If you're ever going to be fit mentally, then you must be optimistic. A person with a positive thinking mentality anticipates happiness, health, and success and believes that he or she can overcome any impediment and hardship.

Moreover, surround yourself with positive people. By surrounding yourself around positive people, you'll hear positive viewpoints, positive stories, and positive affirmations. Negative people are toxic. They are destructive and desire "fear-leaders" not cheerleaders. Negative people rarely visualize a favorable outcome. They always envision that *everything* will go wrong. They are the worst complainers and they are convinced that the whole world is against them.

Do all things without complaining and disputing. - Philippians 2:14

Say *goodbye*, before their negativism consumes you.

Finally, brethren, whatsoever things are true, whatsoever things are honest, whatsoever things are just, whatsoever things are pure, whatsoever things are lovely, whatsoever things are of good

report; if there be any virtue, and if there be any praise, think on these things.
~Philippians 4:8

Paul list things on which we should meditate on; he realized *we choose* what we think about! Sometimes in creating an idea, reaching a goal, or in forming an assumption the right thoughts don't always enter my mind. Whenever I'm up against a challenge, it sometimes seems ridiculous *to see* the bright side. However, I remember it's all about my perspective in these moments that determine my *mental fitness* level.

I've heard many say that a *constant* positive outlook is easier said than done. I concur; however, it's about training your mind to *see* greater. I've learned how to manage the positive and negative and keep them in perspective. Thus, I choose to be optimistic.

You, dear children, are from God and have overcome them, because the one who is in you is greater than the one who is in the world.

~ 1 John 4:4

THE RIGHT COVERING

And take the helmet of salvation... – Ephesians 6:17

Studies have shown that if you are riding a bike or a motorcycle, wearing a helmet can reduce your risk of a serious brain injury and death. Your head is a very important part of your body because it contains your brain, which controls everything in your body.

Just before going into battle, Roman soldiers put on a helmet either made of bronze or of leather with pieces of metal covering it. In addition, it had cheek coverings to protect parts of their faces. Paul, encouraged the church of Ephesus by instructing believers to put on the helmet of salvation to protect themselves while experiencing conflict with the enemy.

Death and life are in the power of the tongue…

~ Proverbs 18:21a

What we say and believe about ourselves determine if we win or lose. We must change the way we talk. Some may think it's insane, let them think that. Every now and then we must give ourselves pep talks. Practice affirming YOURSELF, Say:

I got this!

I'm in it to win it!

I'm coming out on top!

Chapter 5
Better Days Ahead

We all experience rough times, and we wonder, *"if change is coming!"* Our rough experiences serve as tests. God will allow our faith to be tested, it makes us stronger. There have been tests I failed, remember I am fallible! However, because of God's grace, I was enabled to retake the test and pass [learned experiences].

I struggled with my finances. Yes, my mother taught me correctly about the necessity of budgeting and saving, but I learned the hard way, unaware of how my negligence would affect me in my latter years. I suffered by not being able to own something in my own name. It took a while [for me] to decipher wants versus needs.

I wanted to keep up with the latest trends, not realizing I was digging deeper and deeper in debt. My priorities were all discombobulated. Immaturity on any level always places us in a position to grow/learn; *if we recognize the need to grow/learn.*

My credit was *"tore up to the floor up,"* due because I made poor financial decisions. Regardless of *my* underlying reason, I learned that nothing changed until I did things *differently*. Somethings worked and somethings didn't. Still, I kept fighting for the better. I prayed, planned, prioritized, practiced more discipline, and saw fruits of my labor.

If we want to discover better, then we must do better. We all look for better, but better often comes *after* the waiting period. We live in a world of instantaneous gratification. Waiting isn't something we are interested in doing *but* waiting is inevitable.

If we are out shopping, we wait in long lines. If we're in the city during rush hour, we're waiting in traffic. If we're at our favorite fast food restaurant, we have to wait for the person in front of us to order. Waiting *is* unavoidable!

It is amazing that we spend most of our lives waiting on people, waiting for things, and waiting on things we desire. Joseph waited three years in prison before God vindicated him and had him released. Moses waited 80 years before God used him to lead Israel from bondage. David waited from the time of a teenager until he was in his thirties to take over as King of Israel.

The reason so many give up in the process, is because they fail to embody patience. Patience is a part of the process and it is a prerequisite for obtaining your reward. As we face irritations and annoyances, we allow our emotions and sometimes we forfeit what rightfully belongs to us, due to impatience. As followers of Christ, we are called to respond differently *than* the world.

And be not conformed to this world: but be ye transformed by the renewing of your mind, that ye may prove what is that good, and acceptable, and perfect, will of God. ~ Romans 12:2

The Bible calls patience a "fruit of the spirit" (Galatians 5:22). Fruit doesn't grow/ripen overnight. It takes time. The same applies for the fruit of the spirit. It is a process. Patience comes through the various trials we face in our lives.

Job's faith was tested but he didn't become impatient. Abraham, waited patiently until he was an old man and eventually received his promised son. Test and trials are inescapable but so necessary. Patience will get you through tough times and make you stronger.

Man that is born of a woman is of few days and full of trouble. ~ Job 14:1

Nonetheless, if God made you a promise, it's coming to pass… God just puts us on hold *sometimes*. However, God is not slow in keeping His promise(s). While waiting on the promises of God, He utilizes that time in our lives to work on us. Often times we get in a hurry by trying to obtain the bigger things in life. In today's society, money, power, competition, and position are the driving forces of impatience.

"God Works in Our Waiting"

Waiting is foundational. Often times it provides a level of frustration, but it brings transformation. It is during the holding times that He prepares us for the better that is coming. God always has good reasons for making us wait. Waiting is one of God's tools for developing us. Waiting brings out the best and worst in people. Those who have hidden motives won't wait long because they're not interested in the commitment it takes to see something through. They who are committed to the process inhabit success and reap the benefits of their patience.

In my youthful years, I was always so excited around Christmas time. I couldn't wait to put up lights around the house, decorate the tree, and watch ABC's Family 25 Days 'til Christmas movies. On the night of Christmas Eve, I would make a pallet on the floor and attempt to go to bed early. My mom never brought out my gifts until the night of Christmas Eve. It never failed, every year she would bring my gifts out of her trunk around 11:30p.m. I'm sure she thought I was asleep; however, I had one eye closed and the other slightly opened and watched her as placed my gifts underneath the tree. I tossed and turned all night. Around 7 a.m. I excitedly woke up with great anticipation of receiving the things I requested. My mother taught me at a young age… things worth having are always worth the wait!

As we anticipate better, God will sometimes turn up the heat up in our lives just so that we can trust Him the more. While we are waiting on what He has promised us, He utilizes this time to prepare us for *our* better.

But those who trust in the Lord will find new strength. They will soar high on wings like eagles. They will run and not grow weary. They will walk and not faint.

-Isaiah 40:31

"If God said it, count it DONE!"

Chapter 6
Keep Pressing

I press toward the mark of the prize for the high calling of God in Christ Jesus.
Philippians 3:14

Gail Devers, an American retired track and field athlete won the 100-meter dash by only 6/100 of a second over her four top competitors in 1992. While suffering from Grave's disease one year before she won the Olympic gold, she came within two days of having both of her feet amputated. After surviving that scare, she trained and push herself toward the goal. Who would've or could've imagined that the fastest woman in the world was/is the same woman who almost lost her feet. She possessed an Olympic spirit.

Anyone who is focused and determined to win in the Olympics must have faith (believing that he or she will prevail) and proper training (the preparation to prevail). Additionally, they must keep the goal of winning at the forefront of their minds. Those who play professional football, the prize is winning the Super Bowl. Professional golfers' play to win the PGA tournament. Hockey players aim to win the Stanley Cup and Olympic athletes aim to obtain the gold medal. These players train persistently and endure adversity.

The apostle Paul once said in I Corinthians 9:24 (AMP) So run [your race] that you may lay hold [of the prize] and make it yours. Although starting well is important, but finishing well [in God's sight] … bears a more superior implication.

"NO ONE CAN FORCE YOU TO QUIT"

There are some who quit because they don't have what it takes to keep going. Others quit because they don't have the right perspective. People quit because they get overwhelmed. Working in ministry is quite overwhelming [at times]. I can recall a time [during my initial years of pastoring] when I became overwhelmed. I was never taught the meaning of self-care. I neglected my own needs by trying to fulfill the needs of the people. Wisely, I took a sabbatical [for one month] to replenish and restore myself.

Whenever you feel overwhelmed and under pressure, the easiest thing to do is quit! Right, right it is so easy to quit! However, you can get through the overwhelming phase by taking personal time for yourself by doing things that you enjoy.

We are faced with challenges that require decision-making. How we meet our challenges determines our success *or* failure.

There are two types of decisions that we make in life; beneficial or unbeneficial. In our 'bad' decision making, we *usually* quit because we failed to examine our state of awareness. Our contracted awareness caused us to see our outcome negatively. This limits our perspective as our decisions are produced from a place of fear, anxiety, and frustration.

Do you know what's been given to you by God the father? Through His son Jesus, He gave *us* power… POWER to overcome any hardship that life brings. Don't allow LIFE to distract you from this fact!

. The disciple Peter had confidence and courage when he witnessed Jesus walking on the water. Although the sea was rough, he was *still* willing to make those steps because his focus was Jesus. Everything was going well until he began to sink?

Why did Peter sink? Because he took his eyes off of Jesus. What caused Peter to be distracted? He *saw* the boisterous wind and he was frightened. Too often we are discouraged by our perspective…notice the text stated that Peter *saw* the wind, it never said he *felt* it! When the God of peace is present, the chaos that surrounds is irrelevant!

Hebrews 12:2 says, "**Let us fix our eyes on Jesus, the author and finisher of our faith**" (NIV). Christians have a tendency of losing sight of Jesus when focusing on the wrong things. At times like Peter, our fear gets in the way of our faith. God has called us to look forward, not backward. This we do by reaching toward the future, not the past. Keep going even *when* you a mistake because God redemptive Grace restored you *already*.

No matter where we are in life, God has more in store. He never wants us to quit growing. We should always be reach for new heights in our abilities, our spiritual walk, our finances, careers, and our personal relationship(s). No doubt God has already done *enough*… but you haven't seen anything yet!

But as it is written, Eye hath not seen, nor ear heard, neither have entered into the heart of man, the things which God hath prepared for them that love him.
~1 Corinthians 2:9

Yes, we stumble and fall, but if we fix our eyes on Jesus, He will empower us to finish every race, every time!

Chapter 7
Faith Always Wins

According to the National Center for Fathering, more than 20 million children live in a home without the physical presence of a father. Millions more have fathers who are physically present, but emotionally absent. The impact of fatherlessness is visible in our homes, prisons, hospitals, and schools. Each year the percentage of absent fathers increase. African Americans are among the highest. One study shows that seven out of ten high school dropouts are fatherless. Working in education myself, I know several students without present fathers.

I grew up without my biological father as well. Although, I had great and beneficially impactful men in my life that groomed and helped me to become the man I am. One of the men that mentored me was my fifth-grade teacher, Mr. Grady Fischer. He was my first male teacher and it was his first-year teaching after retiring from twenty years of service in the army. He knew I had a calling on my life.

Thus, he has and his wife asked my mother for permission to spend time with me. Without any hesitation my mom agreed, she knew that I would be in good hands. I went everywhere with them. To restaurants, family gatherings, fun factory, golfing, etc., the time I spent with the Fischer family was unforgettable! Eventually, they became one of many godparents I have.

One particular trip we traveled to a lovely cabin. If anyone knows a thing about cabins, you'd know that they are in the woods. We stayed there a few days. As a young African American boy, I'd never heard anything about tubing and I'd never been in water without a visible bottom. While I was in the water, I became quite inquisitive. I asked Uncle Bill and Mr. Fischer if fish and turtles were in the water. Uncle Bill said, "Yes." Then I asked, "Are there snakes in the water?" He responded yes, *again.* My heart began pounding. Finally, I asked, "Are there alligators in the water?" Surprisingly, he responded, yes again. My heart pounded even faster.

I became extremely paranoid and was ready to get out. Thoughts of being eaten by an alligator wrecked my brain. As the minutes passed, I thought *something* was nibbling on my swimming trunks. I SCREAMED for help! "Mr. Fischer, it's an alligator and it's biting me!" He saw my fear and the tears streaming from eyes. As he got closer to me, he nodded his head and laughed [almost uncontrollably]! He said. "Calm down it was only a stick was caught on your swimming trunks!" From that day until now, I told myself that I'd never go tubing again.

Mr. Fischer also took me to Barnes and Nobles quite frequently. I was always excited, not about the books but the caffeine! Forget the books, I thought to myself. Let's go get a Frappuccino and we did just that. Afterwards' I looked through the unique homes magazine and I was mesmerized by the luxurious homes. With all of the time that he invested in me, he taught me how to think and dream big. However, I was *still* missing someone…

If there was ever a mother of the year award, I'd enter my mother's name…*every year*. My mother has always provided educational and spiritual guidance it has served as solid foundation for my salvation and ministry. Being an only child, she couldn't have done it without God. I've shared in the previous chapters some of the lessons that she'd instilled in me… but someone was *still* missing…

There were others who assisted her like my grandparents, uncles, and aunts that took time with me. Many assumed my grandparents were my parents being that I was always around them. My mother's eldest sister took me along with my first cousins to the movies, park, fair, etc., and oh what a time we had… unfortunately, I was *still* missing *him*.

As times passed, I inquired about my biological father. People often said I favored my uncle; but my mom kinda absent-mindedly and frequently said, "Abram, you look like your dad!" My mother never withheld information from me concerning my dad; she simply didn't know his location.

While I was in high school, I decided to search for him. I even searched www.phonebook.com for him unsuccessfully. In my early 20's I signed up for ancestry.com and I was unsuccessful again.

At the beginning of 2017, I started praying for my dad. I knew he was alive, I knew I had siblings, and I felt as though I was close to finding him.

Now faith is the substance of things hoped for, the evidence of things not seen.

-Hebrews 11:1

On Tuesday June 6, 2017, I had a dream that I was following this man around a room. I couldn't see his face, I just remembered him wearing a cap. I tapped him on the shoulder several times, he wouldn't turn around. He then went to this white board and began writing his name:

BYRON JERNINGAN

The name of my father. I knew his however, I had been misspelling his last name. I woke up out of my sleep around 4 a.m. I prayed and thanked God for what *He* revealed to me.

Then I logged on into Facebook and searched for the name that appeared to me in a dream. I clicked on the first profile that appeared. Then I clicked on the profile picture. *There he was…* a dark-skinned man dressed in white. I examined the picture closely for about ten minutes. I knew without a shadow of a doubt that *he was my father.*

Excitedly, I called one of my best friend's and told him my "life-changing" news, I sent him the picture, and he also knew *that was my father.* So, I logged back unto Facebook and sent him a friend request. I waited all day Tuesday to see if he accepted it and I repeated *this wait* on Wednesday. He still had not accepted my request.

On Thursday, I told my aunt about *the* dream and I sent her the picture of my father. She instructed me to go back to his page and to see if any more Jerningans' were listed there. I did just that.

I reached out to who I had discovered to be my first cousin. I asked if she knew a Byron Jerningan. She told me that he was her uncle. I quickly gave her my number and within ten minutes *he* called.

He wanted me to verify my identity, but I didn't release my name. I simply asked if he knew a woman in the late 1980's by the name of Connie. He responded "Yes, I know her; it's been years since I've seen her!" At that moment, I became speechless and there was a pause in our conversation. When I attempted to speak, he stopped me because he instantly knew who I was. My father wasn't absent in my life on purpose, there was miscommunication between him and my mother.

The next day he and his wife along with my siblings drove down from Alabama. Was I upset? Was I angry? Was I bitter? No. The God in me would not allow it and I was just overjoyed in knowing who my father was. Yes, it is true, good things come to those who wait. Until this day my dad and I talk on a weekly basis.

I didn't give up in searching for my father. I stayed in sync with God and He granted my request. Don't give up on God, He cannot fail… and with God, WE won't fail either! Faith ALWAYS wins!

About the Author

Abram Jones is a Florida native. He is an author, mentor, motivational speaker, life coach, and preacher. He is a youthful and positively influential man, that has chosen to humbly serve the body of Christ at large. He's a relevant model for strategic leadership and administration. He attended Luther Rice Christian University and holds a Bachelor of Arts Degree in Christian Counseling.

Abram strives to live on purpose for purpose, because he understands that *his* life is not just for him… but it is for God and His people! Mr. Jones is joyously content to be about His father's business, and he prays daily that the work(s) he does is pleasing to God, edifies the people of God, and that he doesn't grow weary in well-doing!

www.ingramcontent.com/pod-product-compliance
Lightning Source LLC
Chambersburg PA
CBHW051410290426
44108CB00015B/2235